Resurrection Life!
CHELSEA KONG
AF226043

Printed in 2023, Made in Toronto, Canada
ISBN: 978-1-990399-19-0
Library and Archives Canada

HE IS RISEN!
RESURRECTION IS WHEN SOMEBODY WHO DIES BECOMES ALIVE AGAIN.
JESUS CHRIST ROSE FROM THE DEAD.
GOD'S PEOPLE ALSO ARE RAISED FROM THE DEAD.

WE CELEBRATE BY REMEMBERING WHAT CHRIST HAS DONE.
HE IS THE FIRST TO BE RAISED FROM THE DEAD.

HE LIVES FOREVER AND OUR FAITH IN HIM SAVES US.
HE WANTS US TO LIVE WITH GOD FOREVER.

GOD LOVES EVERYONE SO MUCH THAT HE SENT HIS ONLY SON.
JESUS CHRIST CAME TO EARTH TO SAVE EVERYONE.

WE MUST CHOOSE TO HAVE JESUS IN OUR LIFE.
THEN WE CAN BE WITH HIM IN HEAVEN.

JESUS KNOWS WHO WILL FOLLOW HIM.
SOME PEOPLE ONLY WANT HIS BLESSINGS.

MANY WILL HATE GOD AND MAKE FUN OF HIM AND YOU.
PEOPLE WILL HATE US BECAUSE OF JESUS.

PEOPLE CANNOT BE PURE, HOLY, AND RIGHT LIKE GOD.
WE NEED JESUS AND THE HOLY SPIRIT TO HELP US.

NOBODY IS PERFECT BUT ONLY GOD, JESUS, AND HOLY SPIRIT.
LOOK TO JESUS NO MATTER WHAT PEOPLE SAY OR DO.
PRAY FOR THEM TO KNOW JESUS.

HE IS THE ONLY ONE THAT CAN FORGIVE US FROM OUR SINS.
WE NEED TO ASK THEM TO FORGIVE US EVERY DAY WHEN WE SIN.
HE WILL CHANGE US EVERY DAY BY JESUS' BLOOD.

WE BECOME LIKE JESUS MORE AND MORE.
BE BAPTIZED IN WATER WHEN WE CHOOSE HIM.
HOLY SPIRIT WILL ALSO BAPTIZE US WITH HIS POWER AND LATER HIS FIRE.

JESUS TELLS YOU WHO TO TALK WITH.
YOU WILL HAVE NEW FRIENDS.
PRAY, READ THE BIBLE,
AND LISTEN TO GOD.

JESUS GIVES US THE WORDS TO FIGHT THE DEVIL.
HOLY SPIRIT GIVES US POWER TO FIGHT THE DEVIL.

HE IS UNDER OUR FEET, AND WE SHOULD NOT FEAR HIM.

USE THE BIBLE TO FIGHT AGAINST THE DEVIL.
HE HATES JESUS AND ANYONE WHO LOVES JESUS,
HE MAKES YOU SCARED, BUT YOU HAVE ANGELS WITH YOU.
this new girl. is weird

THE DEVIL MADE THE JEWS HATE JESUS AND WANT HIM TO DIE.
THE ROMANS TREATED HIM BADLY AND PUT HIM ON A CROSS TO DIE.
JESUS HAS MANY ANGELS, AND HE OBEYED GOD AND DID WHAT HE SAID.

JESUS LOVES YOU!

JESUS GAVE HIS LIFE FOR US ON THE CROSS.
HE DIED FOR THREE DAYS AFTER PASSOVER.
JESUS IS THE PASSOVER LAMB.

TWO ROBBERS WERE ALSO ON THE CROSS AND ONE CHOSE JESUS.
THE ROMANS GAMBLED FOR JESUS' CLOTHES.
THE DISCIPLES DID NOT UNDERSTAND WHY JESUS HAD TO DIE.

SKY BECAME DARK, AND THE EARTH SHOOK.
JESUS SPOKE LOUDLY AND LEFT HIS BODY ON THE CROSS.
THE VEIL OF THE TEMPLE WAS TORN.

THE CENTURION THEN KNEW JESUS WAS THE SON OF GOD.
AFTER A WHILE LONGER, THEY TOOK JESUS' BODY TO BURY IT.
NICODEMUS AND JOSEPH BURIED HIM IN THE GARDEN TOMB.

JESUS ROSE FROM THE DEAD ON THE THIRD DAY.
HE BROKE THE POWER OF SIN, DEATH, AND HELL.
HE GAVE US BACK THE POWER TO DESTROY THE DEVIL'S WORKS.
Rich man's Garden

THE RESURRECTION MADE MANY WHO DIED COME BACK TO LIFE.
JESUS BRINGS LIFE TO THE DEAD AND TO THE DEAD THINGS.
HE GIVES US COMMAND OVER EVERYTHING TO CHANGE IT FOR GOOD.

JESUS GAVE US A NEW LIFE.
WE WILL ALSO GET A NEW BODY WHEN HE RETURNS AGAIN.
THIS LIFE IS TO LIVE IN HEAVEN AND ON EARTH.

WE WILL ALSO LIVE IN THE NEW HEAVEN, NEW EARTH
WE BECOME HIS BRIDE AND LIVE IN NEW JERUSALEM.
JESUS MAKES A HOME FOR US IN HEAVEN.

THE DEVIL ALWAYS TRIES TO TRICK US AND OTHERS.
WE CAN STOP HIM BEFORE HE ATTACKS US.
WE NEED TO SPEND TIME WITH JESUS AND HE WILL TELL US,

DEVIL

ANGEL

JESUS TOLD HIS DISCIPLES TO SHARE THE GOOD NEWS WITH EVERYONE.
THIS GOOD NEWS IS HIS RESURRECTION FROM THE DEAD.
HE WILL GIVE US MORE THAN WHAT WE NEED.

OBEY AND TRUST IN JESUS ALL THE TIME.
LIFE WILL NOT BE EASY BUT GOD WILL GIVE US REWARDS.
THE DEVIL CANNOT STOP OR DESTROY THOSE WHO STAY IN JESUS.

WE ALSO RULE WITH JESUS IN HEAVEN AND EARTH.
IN JESUS, WE WILL ALWAYS WIN OVER THE DEVIL.
IN JESUS' NAME, WE CAN ASK FOR GREAT THINGS.

JESUS PRAYS FOR US EVERY DAY.
HE HAS A NEW BODY THAT IS LONG LASTING.
JESUS PLEASED GOD ALL THE TIME.

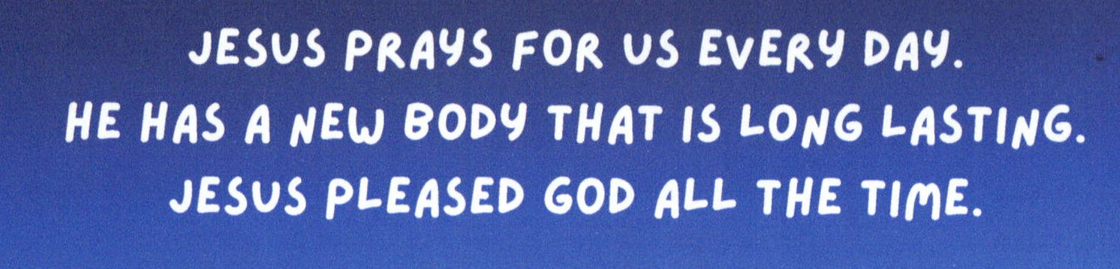

Happy Resurrection Day!

WORSHIP GOD, JESUS, AND THE HOLY SPIRIT.
JESUS IS KING OF KINGS AND LORD OF LORDS.
HE HAS THE POWER TO CHANGE TIMES AND SEASONS.

Garden Tomb

SALVATION PRAYER

God, I know I sinned against you. Forgive me for the wrong that I have done. I believe that Jesus Christ died on the cross for me. That He rose from the grave so that after three days. I can have His long-lasting life. Come into my heart to be my Lord and Savior. I choose to turn away from my sins and I choose to follow you. Lead me to walk with you. Keep me safe and teach me your ways. Stop every bad thing in my life that has an open door to hurt me. Close those doors. Holy Spirit fill me now in Jesus' name. Amen.

BAPTISM IN THE HOLY SPIRIT

Jesus, you are the one that fills me with Your Spirit. Come Holy Spirit and come into my life and fill me to overflow with Your presence. Come with your fire too. Thank you for the gift of tongues in Jesus' name. Amen.

Open your mouth and let the words come out that God gives you. It will be words that you don't know what they mean. You can ask God what it means. You need to let Him talk through you every day to grow this gift.

He will bring you closer to God and you will know Jesus more. You will have power from God to do great things and know things.

Father, thank you for Jesus' life. I would like to thank you for your promises. Thank you for resurrection life. You have the power to change things around me. I would like to thank you for the power over the devil. I would like to thank you for giving me a new life. Thank you for your angels working for me to complete God's plan in my life. Thank you for new friends in Jesus' name. Teach me how to live a holy life for you and be a light for others in Jesus name. Amen.

Message from the Author

We can see Jesus if we ask him to. He wants us to speak in faith and avoid negative words. Jesus spoke only about what God told Him. We need to keep watch over our mouth. The devil uses the wrong words against us and will put thoughts into our mind and heart to make us believe a lie. Jesus also cursed the fig tree because it had no fruit on it. We should not curse others because we will allow the devil to work. He only wants to steal, kill, and destroy. We also should have a life that is full of God's goodness. This will cause others to know that life is better with God. We need to show others that we are different and how good God is. It is not easy but it makes God happy. We will have a better life too.

Knowing God

How to Hear God's Voice

New Life in Jesus

Loving Israel

God's Gifts/Spiritual Talents

Meeting God

Word Power

Fruit of the Spirit

The Tabernacle

Bride for Jesus

A Life of Prayer

Live Free

Who am I in Jesus

Walk in Love

God's Favor

Man of God

Woman of God

How to Use Money

God's Wisdom

Fasting

See Jerusalem and Bethany

First Fruit Offering

Feast of Trumpets

Day of Atonement

Feast of Tabernacles

Counting the Omer

Festival of Lights

See Galilee, Nazareth, and Tiberias

Pentecost

Glory, Presence, and Holy Spirit

Live in God's Presence

31 Day Devotional

Biblical Puzzle Book Vol 1-5

Bible Puzzles for Young Children Book 1-3

Biblical Puzzle for Children Books 1-3

Hear God Speak

Knowing Jesus

Knowing Holy Spirit

A Healthy Life and A Healthy Life Work Book

Smokey the Cat

Passover Unleavened Bread

Teaching Series

How to Hear God's Voice Teaching Guide & Audio Book

Relationship with God, Jesus, Holy Spirit Guide

Knowing God, Jesus, Holy Spirit Guide & Audio Book

Flowing in the Prophetic

Teaching (Non-Sale on my website)

Purim

Passover

Resurrection

More books to come!

More books on Amazon, Kobo, and Barnes and Noble, and Smashwords.

https://chelseak532002550.wordpress.com/

Review

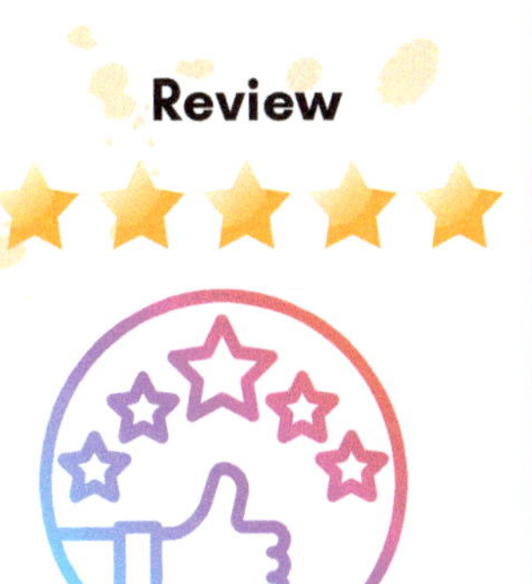

More books on Amazon, Kobo, and Barnes and Noble, and Smashwords

https://www.amazon.com/author/chelseakong

Please leave a review and share with friends to help the author continue to write more books to reach more readers. Thank you so much for your support.

About
CHELSEA KONG

She is a writer, creative arts and digital media artist, skilled administration professional, and podcaster. Chelsea also served in a variety of roles, from audiovisual, photography, to assisting on the worship team, and ministry team. She also has a passion for families being united.

Chelsea has been a guest on Unity Live Radio and The Lady Tracey Show and is highly recommended by a Proud Christian blog. She graduated from Hotel and Restaurant Management, Digital Media Arts, Office Administration, and experience working with children. Chelsea lives in Toronto, Canada. She mainly writes children's books, stories, bridal writing, poems, lyrics for songs, words of encouragement, blessings, prayers, and jokes. The author of How to Hear the Voice of God, the Bridal Collection, Knowing God, etc. She also has her own Bible Puzzle books and other inspired products. Her podcast channel is called Chelsea K on Anchor, Spotify, and iTunes.

Please check my website to find out more:
https://chelseak532002550.wordpress.com/

www.ingramcontent.com/pod-product-compliance
Lightning Source LLC
Chambersburg PA
CBHW042155030726
47599CB00004B/740